WINE

MAKES MUMMY CLEVER

HODDER &
STOUGHTON

ANDY RILEY IS THE AUTHOR/ARTIST OF THE BOOK OF BUNNY SUICIDES, DAWN OF THE BUNNY SUICIDES AND EVERY OTHER BUNNY SUICIDE THING. HIS OTHER BOOKS INCLUDE GREAT LIES TO TELL SMALL KIDS, LOADS MORE LIES TO TELL SMALL KIDS, SELFISH PIGS, ROASTED AND D.I.Y. DENTISTRY.

HIS SCRIPTWRITING WORK INCLUDES BLACK BOOKS, THE GREAT OUTDOORS, HYPERDRIVE, LITTLE BRITAIN, ARMSTRONG AND MILLER, GNOMEO & JULIET, THE ARMANDO IANNUCCI SHOWS, HARRY+PAUL, SLACKER CATS AND THE BAFTA-WINNING ANIMATION ROBBIE THE REINDEER.

misterandyriley.com

FIRST PUBLISHED IN GREAT BRITAIN IN 2010 BY
HODDER AND STOUGHTON, AN HACHETTE UK COMPANY

1

HARDBACK ISBN 978 1 444 71103 5

PRINTED & BOUND IN ITALY BY L.E.G.O. SPA

HODDER & STOUGHTON POLICY IS TO USE PAPERS MADE
FROM WOOD GROWN IN SUSTAINABLE FORESTS.
THE LOGGING & MANUFACTURING PROCESSES ARE
EXPECTED TO CONFORM TO THE ENVIRONMENTAL
REGULATIONS OF THE COUNTRY OF ORIGIN.

HODDER AND STOUGHTON 338 EUSTON ROAD,
LONDON NW1 3BH
WWW. HODDER.CO.UK

WITH THANKS TO:
GORDON WISE, LISA HIGHTON
AND ALL AT HODDER, POLLY
FABER AND KEVIN CECIL.

OTHER PEOPLE'S TODDLERS

MAKE MUMMY NOT
WANT ANOTHER ONE

MUM'S LAW OF LIPSTICK:

WHOEVER DIES WITH THE MOST COLOURS WINS

CHOCOLATE CAKE

MUMMY KNOWS
IT'S WRONG

BUT IT FEELS
SO RIGHT

WEBSITES
ABOUT
MOTHERING

GIVE MUM TIPS TO BE A BETTER PARENT

AND HELP HER IGNORE THE KIDS
FOR TWENTY MINUTES

ALL AT THE SAME TIME

"I WILL SURVIVE"

MUMMY CAN'T
NOT DANCE
TO IT

MAKES MUMMY'S
MORNING
MAGICALLY
VANISH

THE SMELL OF SUN BLOCK

MAKES MUMMY
FEEL LIKE SHE'S ON
HOLIDAY ALREADY

MUFFINS

MUMMY'S "EARNED ONE"

ROUND ABOUT 4 PM
EVERY DAY

MUMMY'S FINGER

DON'T MAKE IT WAG

TOO LATE!
IT'S WAGGING

EX-BOYFRIENDS

MAKE MUMMY
FEEL AWKWARD

YET SOMEHOW
STILL ADMIRED

KILLER HEELS

NO, MUMMY'S NOT TOO OLD TO WEAR THEM

KILLED

(MUMMY THE DAY
AFTER THE
KILLER HEELS)

FASHION MISTAKES

MUMMY KEEPS
THEM IN THE
BOTTOM DRAWER
OF SHAME

THE WEDDING DRESS

YES, MUMMY COULD
STILL FIT INTO IT

SHE'S JUST NOT GOING
TO TRY IT TODAY, IS ALL

RICE CAKES

ONE DAY MUMMY WILL
CONVINCE HER STOMACH
THAT THEY MAKE A
SATISFYING MEAL

AND THEN EVERYTHING
WILL BE FINE

THE
BATH

MAKES MUMMY
≷ DISAPPEAR ≷
FOR UP TO AN HOUR

DAYTIME TELLY

MUM TRIES TO
RATION HERSELF

NO MORE THAN
NINE HOURS A DAY

FLOWERS

IF THEY'VE BEEN BOUGHT
FROM A GARAGE

MUMMY CAN *ALWAYS TELL*

CLEANING

NO-ONE NOTICES IT HAPPENS

UNTIL MUMMY GOES
AWAY FOR TWO DAYS

MINIBREAK

MUMMY NEEDS ONE
NOW

MORE
CHOCOLATE CAKE

" THE SOONER IT'S ALL GONE,
THE SOONER IT'S NOT THERE
TO TEMPT ME "

THAT'S MUMMY'S REASONING

MUMMY
SPIT

REMOVES ALL
KNOWN STAINS

THE GYM

MUMMY'S STILL
A MEMBER

THE 5 SIGNS OF PROBLEM HAIR

MUMMY THINKS
SHE'S GOT 7 OR
8 OF THEM

HOROSCOPES

♎ ♐ ♈ ♋ ♓ ♌ ♏

travel and adventure beckon

financial worries loom

MUMMY KNOWS TO
IGNORE THE BAD ONES

AND TRUST THE
GOOD ONES

DIRTY DANCING

MUMMY'S SEEN IT _ _ _ TIMES

↑

(INSERT CORRECT
NUMBER
HERE)

RECESSION OR
NO RECESSION
MUMMY NEEDS ONE

SPA TREATMENTS

MUMMY LOVES THEM ESPECIALLY WHEN MUMMY'S NOT PAYING

YET MORE
CHOCOLATE CAKE

LOOK, JUST GIVE
IT TO MUMMY
NOW, OKAY?

SOCKS
IN BED

NOT VERY SEXY

BUT MUM'S GOT
TO KEEP WARM

MUM'S STOPPED MAKING
JOKES ABOUT CELEBRITIES
WHO'VE HAD IT DONE

SOMETHING'S UP

MUM'S POSH SHAMPOO

SOMEONE'S BEEN USING
IT AS *SHOWER GEL* AGAIN

SOMEONE'S GOING
TO GET **KILLED**

SHOES

ARE SOMETHING
MUMMY WILL
DEFINITELY ORGANISE
THIS WEEKEND,
DEFINITELY

SWIMMER'S SHOULDERS

PEOPLE SOMETIMES SAY
MUMMY HAS THEM

SHE'S STILL TRYING TO
WORK OUT IF IT'S A
COMPLIMENT OR NOT

HEN NIGHTS

MAKE MUMMY FEEL EIGHTEEN

GRAND CHILDREN

...MUMMY'S PAYOFF
FOR ALL THAT
HARD WORK

ICE CREAM

MUMMY'S DOWNFALL
(WHEN THERE'S NO
CHOCOLATE CAKE LEFT)

AND

AND !!

REFILL
REQUIRED